THE
CONSTITUTION
OF THE
UNITED STATES
OF AMERICA

PLAIN ENGLISH
TRANSLATION

constitution-in-plain-english.com

Dedicated to those who turn words into action.

ISBN-13: 978-1542401388

Printed in the United States of America.

Second Edition.

Book design by K. Lawson

Cover design by K. Lawson

For more information,
please email info@opinfoprod.com

Contents

* Text highlighted in gray was altered by Amendment.

Preamble

We the People of the United States, in Order to form a more perfect Union, establish Justice, insure domestic Tranquility, provide for the common defence, promote the general Welfare, and secure the Blessings of Liberty to ourselves and our Posterity, do ordain and establish this Constitution for the United States of America.

Preamble

We the People of the United States officially establish this Constitution for the United States of America. We did this to form a more perfect Union, one that is just and peaceful. We did this to protect each other, and to make each other healthier and happier. We did this to ensure freedom for ourselves and all that follow.

Article I.

Article 1.
The Congress.

Section 1.

All legislative Powers herein granted shall be vested in a Congress of the United States, which shall consist of a Senate and House of Representatives.

Section 2.

The House of Representatives shall be composed of Members chosen every second Year by the People of the several States, and the Electors in each State shall have the Qualifications requisite for Electors of the most numerous Branch of the State Legislature.

No Person shall be a Representative who shall not have attained to the Age of twenty five Years, and been seven Years a Citizen of the United States, and who shall not, when elected, be an Inhabitant of that State in which he shall be chosen.

Section 1. *Grant of Power and Structure.*

All law-making Powers under this Constitution belong to a Congress of the United States. Congress is made up of a Senate and House of Representatives.

Section 2. *The House of Representatives.*

The House of Representative is made up of members elected for two-year terms by the people of their State. Those people who meet the requirements to vote for the largest branch of their State Legislature are qualified to vote for their Representatives.

No one can be a Representative of a State unless they:

- are at least twenty-five years old, and
- a United States citizen for at least seven years, and
- are living in that State when elected.

Section 2. (cont.)

Representatives and direct Taxes shall be apportioned among the several States which may be included within this Union, according to their respective Numbers, which shall be determined by adding to the whole Number of free Persons, including those bound to Service for a Term of Years, and excluding Indians not taxed, three fifths of all other Persons. The actual Enumeration shall be made within three Years after the first Meeting of the Congress of the United States, and within every subsequent Term of ten Years, in such Manner as they shall by Law direct.

Section 2. (cont.)

Each State gets Representatives and direct taxes in proportion to its population. A State's population is calculated
by first counting all free people, including indentured ser-
vants but excluding non-citizen Indians under tribal rule.
That number is then added to three-fifths of the number of
slaves in that State. Amendment 14, ratified July 28, 1868

The first Census will be held within three years after the
first meeting of Congress to calculate each State's population. After that, each State's population will be calculated every ten years as Congress directs by Law.

Section 2. (cont.)

The Number of Representatives shall not exceed one for every thirty Thousand, but each State shall have at Least one Representative; and until such enumeration shall be made, the State of New Hampshire shall be entitled to chuse three, Massachusetts eight, Rhode-Island and Providence Plantations one, Connecticut five, New-York six, New Jersey four, Pennsylvania eight, Delaware one, Maryland six, Virginia ten, North Carolina five, South Carolina five, and Georgia three.

When vacancies happen in the Representation from any State, the Executive Authority thereof shall issue Writs of Election to fill such Vacancies.

The House of Representatives shall chuse their Speaker and other Officers; and shall have the sole Power of Impeachment.

Section 2. (cont.)

The House can have no more Representatives than one for every 30,000 people. Each State gets at least one Representative.

Until the first Census, each State gets the following number of Representatives:

- New Hampshire - 3
- Massachusetts - 8
- Rhode Island and the Providence Plantations - 1
- Connecticut - 5
- New York - 6
- New Jersey - 4
- Pennsylvania - 8
- Delaware - 1
- Maryland - 6
- Virginia - 10
- North Carolina - 5
- South Carolina - 5
- Georgia - 3

The Governor of a State will order an Election whenever that State has a vacancy in the House.

The House chooses their Speaker and other officers.

The House alone can impeach.

Section 3.

The Senate of the United States shall be composed of two Senators from each State, chosen by the Legislature thereof, for six Years; and each Senator shall have one Vote.

Immediately after they shall be assembled in Consequence of the first Election, they shall be divided as equally as may be into three Classes. The Seats of the Senators of the first Class shall be vacated at the Expiration of the second Year, of the second Class at the Expiration of the fourth Year, and of the third Class at the Expiration of the sixth Year, so that one third may be chosen every second Year; and if Vacancies happen by Resignation, or otherwise, during the Recess of the Legislature of any State, the Executive thereof may make temporary Appointments until the next Meeting of the Legislature, which shall then fill such Vacancies.

No Person shall be a Senator who shall not have attained to the Age of thirty Years, and been nine Years a Citizen of the United States, and who shall not, when elected, be an Inhabitant of that State for which he shall be chosen.

The Vice President of the United States shall be President of the Senate, but shall have no Vote, unless they be equally divided.

Section 3. *The Senate.*

The Senate of the United States is made up of Senators elected for six-year terms by the Legislature of their State. Each State gets two Senators. Each Senator has one vote. Amendment 17, ratified April 8, 1913

After the first Election under this Constitution, the first Senate will assemble and be divided equally into three Classes. Senators in Class 1 will serve for two years after the first Election. Senators in Class 2 will serve for four years. Senators in Class 3 will serve for six years. This is done so that one-third of the Senate is elected every two years.

If a State has a vacancy in the Senate during the Recess of that State's Legislature, the Governor of that State can temporarily appoint a Senator. The next time the State Legislature meets, they will fill the vacancy. Amendment 17, ratified April 8, 1913

No one can be a Senator of a State unless they:

- are thirty years old, and
- a United States citizen for at least nine-years, and
- are living in that State when elected.

The Vice President is the President of the Senate. He cannot vote unless there is a tie.

Section 3. (cont.)

The Senate shall chuse their other Officers, and also a President pro tempore, in the Absence of the Vice President, or when he shall exercise the Office of President of the United States.

The Senate shall have the sole Power to try all Impeachments. When sitting for that Purpose, they shall be on Oath or Affirmation. When the President of the United States is tried, the Chief Justice shall preside: And no Person shall be convicted without the Concurrence of two thirds of the Members present.

Judgment in Cases of Impeachment shall not extend further than to removal from Office, and disqualification to hold and enjoy any Office of honor, Trust or Profit under the United States: but the Party convicted shall nevertheless be liable and subject to Indictment, Trial, Judgment and Punishment, according to Law.

Section 4.

The Times, Places and Manner of holding Elections for Senators and Representatives, shall be prescribed in each State by the Legislature thereof; but the Congress may at any time by Law make or alter such Regulations, except as to the Places of chusing Senators.

Section 3. (cont.)

The Senate chooses their officers and a President pro tempore. The President pro tempore is the President of the Senate when the Vice President is absent or when he becomes Acting President or President.

The Senate tries impeachment cases. Senators must swear to run the trial fairly. The Chief Justice of the Supreme Court must be the judge when the President is on trial. No one can be convicted without a two-thirds vote of the members present.

The only punishments in impeachment trials are removal from office and disqualification from holding Federal office. Those convicted can still be held responsible in court and be indicted, tried, judged and punished under the Law.

Section 4. *Congressional Elections.*

The rules for when, where and how Elections for Senators and Representatives are held in each State will be decided by that State's Legislature. At any time, Congress can make or alter those rules by Law, except as to where State Legislatures choose their Senators.

Section 4. (cont.)

The Congress shall assemble at least once in every Year, and such Meeting shall be on the first Monday in December, unless they shall by Law appoint a different Day.

Section 5.

Each House shall be the Judge of the Elections, Returns and Qualifications of its own Members, and a Majority of each shall constitute a Quorum to do Business; but a smaller Number may adjourn from day to day, and may be authorized to compel the Attendance of absent Members, in such Manner, and under such Penalties as each House may provide.

Each House may determine the Rules of its Proceedings, punish its Members for disorderly Behaviour, and, with the Concurrence of two thirds, expel a Member.

Each House shall keep a Journal of its Proceedings, and from time to time publish the same, excepting such Parts as may in their Judgment require Secrecy; and the Yeas and Nays of the Members of either House on any question shall, at the Desire of one fifth of those Present, be entered on the Journal.

Section 4. (cont.)

Congress must meet at least once a year. That meeting must be on first Monday in December. Congress can choose a different day by Law. ^{Amendment 20, ratified January 23, 1933}

Section 5. *Bylaws.*

Each House judges the Elections, election returns, and qualifications of its own members. A majority of each House is required to start a Session. A smaller number can meet and adjourn from day to day, and force absent members to attend. Each House decides how to force attendance and the penalties for not attending.

Each House decides its own rules and how to punish its members for breaking them. Each House can remove a member with a two-thirds vote.

Each House keeps a Journal and must publish it from time to time. Each House may redact parts they decide must be kept secret. The votes of the members of either House on any question must be recorded in the Journal if one-fifth of the members present vote to do so.

Section 5. (cont.)

Neither House, during the Session of Congress, shall, without the Consent of the other, adjourn for more than three days, nor to any other Place than that in which the two Houses shall be sitting.

Section 6.

The Senators and Representatives shall receive a Compensation for their Services, to be ascertained by Law, and paid out of the Treasury of the United States. They shall in all Cases, except Treason, Felony and Breach of the Peace, be privileged from Arrest during their Attendance at the Session of their respective Houses, and in going to and returning from the same; and for any Speech or Debate in either House, they shall not be questioned in any other Place.

No Senator or Representative shall, during the Time for which he was elected, be appointed to any civil Office under the Authority of the United States, which shall have been created, or the Emoluments whereof shall have been encreased during such time; and no Person holding any Office under the United States, shall be a Member of either House during his Continuance in Office.

Section 5. (cont.)

During a Session, neither House can adjourn for more than three days without the approval of the other.

During a Session, neither House can adjourn to any other place than where the two Houses are meeting without the approval of the other.

Section 6. *Compensation.*

Senators and Representatives are paid for their services. The amount is decided by Law and paid out of the United States Treasury.

Senators and Representatives have immunity from civil arrest, but not criminal arrest, when attending, going to, or leaving a Session of their House. They have absolute immunity for any speech or debate in either House.

No Senator or Representative can be appointed as a civil Federal official if, during their time in office:

- that position was created, or
- the pay for that position was increased.

No member of either House can be a Federal official during their time in office.

Section 7.

All Bills for raising Revenue shall originate in the House of Representatives; but the Senate may propose or concur with Amendments as on other Bills.

Every Bill which shall have passed the House of Representatives and the Senate, shall, before it become a Law, be presented to the President of the United States; If he approve he shall sign it, but if not he shall return it, with his Objections to that House in which it shall have originated, who shall enter the Objections at large on their Journal, and proceed to reconsider it. If after such Reconsideration two thirds of that House shall agree to pass the Bill, it shall be sent, together with the Objections, to the other House, by which it shall likewise be reconsidered, and if approved by two thirds of that House, it shall become a Law. But in all such Cases the Votes of both Houses shall be determined by yeas and Nays, and the Names of the Persons voting for and against the Bill shall be entered on the Journal of each House respectively. If any Bill shall not be returned by the President within ten Days (Sundays excepted) after it shall have been presented to him, the Same shall be a Law, in like Manner as if he had signed it, unless the Congress by their Adjournment prevent its Return, in which Case it shall not be a Law.

Section 7. *Presentment.*

Bills for raising revenue must be introduced in the House of Representatives. The Senate can propose and vote on Amendments to those Bills as they can on any other Bill.

Every Bill passed by both the House of Representatives and the Senate must be presented to the President of the United States before it becomes a Law. If he approves the Bill, he signs it and it becomes a Law. If not, he may Veto it by returning it to the House that introduced the Bill with his objections. That House records his objections in their Journal and reconsiders the Bill. That House can pass the Bill again with a two-thirds vote. The Bill is then sent to the other House together with the President's objections. The other House can pass the bill again with a two-thirds vote. If the Bill passes both houses in this way, the Veto is overridden and the Bill becomes a Law.

All Bills are voted on and decided by Yes and No votes. The names of the persons voting for and against the Bill are recorded in the Journal of that House.

If a Bill is not returned by the President within ten days (excluding Sundays) after it was presented to him, that Bill becomes a Law as if he had signed it. It does not become a Law if Congress adjourned to prevent him from returning the Bill to them.

Section 7. (cont.)

Every Order, Resolution, or Vote to which the Concurrence of the Senate and House of Representatives may be necessary (except on a question of Adjournment) shall be presented to the President of the United States; and before the Same shall take Effect, shall be approved by him, or being disapproved by him, shall be repassed by two thirds of the Senate and House of Representatives, according to the Rules and Limitations prescribed in the Case of a Bill.

Section 8.

The Congress shall have Power To lay and collect Taxes, Duties, Imposts and Excises, to pay the Debts and provide for the common Defence and general Welfare of the United States; but all Duties, Imposts and Excises shall be uniform throughout the United States;

To borrow Money on the credit of the United States;

To regulate Commerce with foreign Nations, and among the several States, and with the Indian Tribes;

Section 7. (cont.)

Every order, resolution, or vote that requires approval of both the Senate and the House of Representatives must be presented to the President of the United States, except for a vote to adjourn. The President must approve that order, resolution, or vote before it can take effect. If he does not, it must be repassed by a two-thirds vote of the Senate and the House of Representatives under the same requirements for passing a Bill.

Section 8. *Powers of Congress.*

Congress has the power:

- to impose and collect taxes, duties, imposts, and excises to pay the debts of, and to provide for the protection and welfare of the United States. All duties, imposts, and excises must be uniform throughout the United States.

- to borrow money on the credit of the United States.

- to regulate commerce with foreign countries, between the States, and with the Indian Tribes.

Section 8. (cont.)

To establish an uniform Rule of Naturalization, and uniform Laws on the subject of Bankruptcies throughout the United States;

To coin Money, regulate the Value thereof, and of foreign Coin, and fix the Standard of Weights and Measures;

To provide for the Punishment of counterfeiting the Securities and current Coin of the United States;

To establish Post Offices and post Roads;

To promote the Progress of Science and useful Arts, by securing for limited Times to Authors and Inventors the exclusive Right to their respective Writings and Discoveries;

To constitute Tribunals inferior to the supreme Court;

To define and punish Piracies and Felonies committed on the high Seas, and Offences against the Law of Nations;

To raise and support Armies, but no Appropriation of Money to that Use shall be for a longer Term than two Years;

To provide and maintain a Navy;

Section 8. (cont.)

- to make a nationwide rule for becoming a United States citizen.
- to make nationwide bankruptcy rules.

- to print money and regulate its value.
- to regulate the value of foreign currencies.
- to decide standard units of measurement.
- to decide the punishment for counterfeiting the securities and currency of the United States.

- to establish Post Offices, and create and designate Post Roads.
- to promote science and the arts, by giving exclusive rights for limited times to authors and inventors in their writings and discoveries.

- to create the lower Courts to the Supreme Court.

- to criminalize piracy and felonies committed at sea.
- to criminalize violations of international law.

- to raise and support armies. No law can allocate money for that use for longer than a two-year term.

- to form and maintain a navy.

Section 8. (cont.)

To make Rules for the Government and Regulation of the land and naval Forces;

To provide for calling forth the Militia to execute the Laws of the Union, suppress Insurrections and repel Invasions;

To declare War, grant Letters of Marque and Reprisal, and make Rules concerning Captures on Land and Water;

To provide for organizing, arming, and disciplining, the Militia, and for governing such Part of them as may be employed in the Service of the United States, reserving to the States respectively, the Appointment of the Officers, and the Authority of training the Militia according to the discipline prescribed by Congress;

Section 8. (cont.)

- to make the rules for the military and its legal system.

- to call the State Militias into service to enforce Federal law, suppress rebellions, and defend against invasions.

- to declare war.
- to license private citizens to seize enemy property.
- to make rules about how enemy property is seized and disposed.

- to organize, arm and train the State Militias and arrange uniform command over those Militias called into service of the United States. Each State reserves the power to appoint the officers of its Militia. Each State reserves the power to train its Militia under the rules set by Congress.

Section 8. (cont.)

To exercise exclusive Legislation in all Cases whatsoever, over such District (not exceeding ten Miles square) as may, by Cession of particular States, and the Acceptance of Congress, become the Seat of the Government of the United States, and to exercise like Authority over all Places purchased by the Consent of the Legislature of the State in which the Same shall be, for the Erection of Forts, Magazines, Arsenals, dock-Yards, and other needful Buildings; — And

To make all Laws which shall be necessary and proper for carrying into Execution the foregoing Powers, and all other Powers vested by this Constitution in the Government of the United States, or in any Department or Officer thereof.

Section 9.

The Migration or Importation of such Persons as any of the States now existing shall think proper to admit, shall not be prohibited by the Congress prior to the Year one thousand eight hundred and eight, but a Tax or duty may be imposed on such Importation, not exceeding ten dollars for each Person.

Section 8. (cont.)

- to make laws of any kind over the District designated as the United States capitol. This District may be created on land that is given by particular States and accepted by Congress. This land cannot be larger than ten square miles.
- to make laws of any kind over land purchased from a State for Federal purposes such as military bases and other necessary buildings. This applies only if the purchase of that land is approved by that State's Legislature.
- to pass laws necessary and proper for carrying out the powers listed here and all others granted to the Federal government or any Department or Federal official by this Constitution.

Section 9. *Limits on the Federal Government.*

The Federal government cannot:

- ban the importation of slaves into currently existing States where slavery is legal before the year 1808. Congress may tax the importation of slaves. That tax cannot be higher than ten dollars per slave. Amendment 13, ratified December 6, 1865

Section 9. (cont.)

The Privilege of the Writ of Habeas Corpus shall not be suspended, unless when in Cases of Rebellion or Invasion the public Safety may require it.

No Bill of Attainder or ex post facto Law shall be passed.

No Capitation, or other direct, Tax shall be laid, unless in Proportion to the Census or Enumeration herein before directed to be taken.

No Tax or Duty shall be laid on Articles exported from any State.

No Preference shall be given by any Regulation of Commerce or Revenue to the Ports of one State over those of another; nor shall Vessels bound to, or from, one State, be obliged to enter, clear, or pay Duties in another.

No Money shall be drawn from the Treasury, but in Consequence of Appropriations made by Law; and a regular Statement and Account of the Receipts and Expenditures of all public Money shall be published from time to time.

Section 9. (cont.)

* prevent Courts from ordering the release of prison-ers held illegally or for no legal reason, except during rebellion or invasion.

* pass laws that convict and punish a person or group of people of a crime without trial.
* pass laws that make illegal an act that was legal when committed.
* impose a direct tax, except in proportion to population as calculated under this Constitution. Amendment 16, ratified February 3, 1913

* tax items exported from any State.

* pass laws or impose taxes that discriminate in favor of the ports of one State over another. This includes requiring ships entering or leaving one State to stop in, pass through, or pay taxes in another.

* spend money from the Treasury, except where that money is allocated by Law. A regular report account-ing for all public money collected and spent must be published from time to time.

Section 9. (cont.)

No Title of Nobility shall be granted by the United States: And no Person holding any Office of Profit or Trust under them, shall, without the Consent of the Congress, accept of any present, Emolument, Office, or Title, of any kind whatever, from any King, Prince, or foreign State.

Section 10.

No State shall enter into any Treaty, Alliance, or Confederation; grant Letters of Marque and Reprisal; coin Money; emit Bills of Credit; make any Thing but gold and silver Coin a Tender in Payment of Debts; pass any Bill of Attainder, ex post facto Law, or Law impairing the Obligation of Contracts, or grant any Title of Nobility.

Section 9. (cont.)

- grant any title of nobility. No Federal official can accept any present, payment or gains, office, or title of any kind from any King, Prince, or foreign country, without approval from Congress.

Section 10. *Limits on the States.*

States cannot:

- enter into any treaty, alliance, or coalition with foreign countries.
- grant licenses to capture enemy vessels for private gain.
- print money.
- allow anything other than gold- or silver-backed money to be used as legal tender.
- pass laws that convict and punish a person or group of people of a crime without trial.
- pass laws that make illegal an act that was legal when committed.
- pass laws that interfere with existing contracts.
- grant any title of nobility.

Section 10. (cont.)

No State shall, without the Consent of the Congress, lay any Imposts or Duties on Imports or Exports, except what may be absolutely necessary for executing it's inspection Laws; and the net Produce of all Duties and Imposts, laid by any State on Imports or Exports, shall be for the Use of the Treasury of the United States; and all such Laws shall be subject to the Revision and Controul of the Congress.

No State shall, without the Consent of Congress, lay any Duty of Tonnage, keep Troops, or Ships of War in time of Peace, enter into any Agreement or Compact with another State, or with a foreign Power, or engage in War, unless actually invaded, or in such imminent Danger as will not admit of delay.

Section 10. (cont.)

States cannot, without approval from Congress:

- tax imports or exports, except as absolutely necessary to enforcing that State's inspection laws. If they
impose an import or export tax, the United States
Treasury claims any profits collected. Laws imposing
those taxes can be changed and controlled by Congress.

- tax people or ships for using their ports.
- keep a standing army or navy during peacetime.
- enter into contracts or treaties with other States or
foreign countries.
- wage war, unless actually invaded or threatened with
immediate danger.

Article II.

Article 2.
The President.

Section 1.

The executive Power shall be vested in a President of the United States of America. He shall hold his Office during the Term of four Years, and, together with the Vice President, chosen for the same Term, be elected, as follows:

Each State shall appoint, in such Manner as the Legislature thereof may direct, a Number of Electors, equal to the whole Number of Senators and Representatives to which the State may be entitled in the Congress: but no Senator or Representative, or Person holding an Office of Trust or Profit under the United States, shall be appointed an Elector.

The Electors shall meet in their respective States, and vote by Ballot for two Persons, of whom one at least shall not be an Inhabitant of the same State with themselves. And they shall make a List of all the Persons voted for, and of the Number of Votes for each; which List they shall sign and certify, and transmit sealed to the Seat of the Government of the United States, directed to the President of the Senate. The President of the Senate shall, in the Presence of the Senate and House of Representatives, open all the Certificates, and the Votes shall then be counted.

Section 1. *Grant of Power and Elections.*

The Power to enforce the laws belongs to the President, who serves for a four-year term. The Vice President serves during the same term. The President and Vice President are elected in the following way:

Each State appoints Electors. The State Legislature of each State decides how that State appoints its Electors. Each State gets a number of Electors equal to its total number of Senators and Representatives in Congress. A Senator, Representative, or other Federal official cannot be appointed as an Elector.

The Electors meet in their States, and each Elector votes for two people. At least one of those people must live in a different State than that Elector. The Electors of each State then make a list of how many votes each person got. Then, the Electors sign the list and mail it to the President of the Senate at the capitol of the United States.

The President of the Senate will open the list and count the votes. This will be done in front of the Senate and House of Representatives. Amendment 12, ratified June 15, 1804

Section 1. (cont.)

The Person having the greatest Number of Votes shall be
the President, if such Number be a Majority of the whole
Number of Electors appointed; and if there be more than
one who have such Majority, and have an equal Number
of Votes, then the House of Representatives shall immediately chuse by Ballot one of them for President; and if
no Person have a Majority, then from the five highest on
the List the said House shall in like Manner chuse the
President. But in chusing the President, the Votes shall be
taken by States, the Representation from each State having one Vote; a quorum for this Purpose shall consist of a
Member or Members from two thirds of the States, and a
Majority of all the States shall be necessary to a Choice.
In every Case, after the Choice of the President, the Person having the greatest Number of Votes of the Electors
shall be the Vice President. But if there should remain
two or more who have equal Votes, the Senate shall chuse
from them by Ballot the Vice President.

Section 1. (cont.)

The person who gets votes from a majority of the Electors, and gets more votes than anyone else, becomes President. If more than one person gets votes from a majority of the Electors, and each of those people got the same number of votes, then the House of Representatives selects the President from among those people. If no one gets votes from a majority of the Electors, then the House of Representatives selects the President from among the five people who got the most votes.

Where the House of Representatives selects the President, it must do so by majority vote. The vote is held by State, and the Representatives of a State together have one vote. Representatives from at least two-thirds of the States must be present for the vote. The person who gets votes from a majority of the States becomes President.

After the President is elected, the person who gets more votes from the Electors than anyone else becomes Vice President. If there is a tie between two or more people, then the Senate selects the Vice President. Amendment 12, ratified June 15, 1804

Section 1. (cont.)

The Congress may determine the Time of chusing the Electors, and the Day on which they shall give their Votes; which Day shall be the same throughout the United States.

No Person except a natural born Citizen, or a Citizen of the United States, at the time of the Adoption of this Constitution, shall be eligible to the Office of President; neither shall any Person be eligible to that Office who shall not have attained to the Age of thirty five Years, and been fourteen Years a Resident within the United States.

In Case of the Removal of the President from Office, or of his Death, Resignation, or Inability to discharge the Powers and Duties of the said Office, the Same shall devolve on the Vice President, and the Congress may by Law provide for the Case of Removal, Death, Resignation or Inability, both of the President and Vice President, declaring what Officer shall then act as President, and such Officer shall act accordingly, until the Disability be removed, or a President shall be elected.

The President shall, at stated Times, receive for his Services, a Compensation, which shall neither be increased nor diminished during the Period for which he shall have been elected, and he shall not receive within that Period any other Emolument from the United States, or any of them.

Section 1. (cont.)

Congress decides when Electors are chosen and when they vote. They must vote on the same day throughout the United States.

No one can be President unless they:

- are a natural born citizen, or a citizen when this Constitution goes into effect, and
- are at least thirty-five years old, and
- lived in the United States for at least fourteen years.

If the President is removed from office, dies, resigns, or is unable to carry out the responsibilities of President, the Vice President becomes President. Congress can decide by Law which official becomes Acting President if both the President and Vice President are removed from office, die, resign, or are unable to carry out their responsibilities. That offical will be Acting President until the President or Vice President is not unable to carry out the responsibilities of President or until a new President is elected.
Amendment 25, ratified February 10, 1967

The President is paid for his services. The amount paid will not increase or decrease during his term. The President will not get any other payments or gains from the United States or any State.

Section 1. (cont.)

Before he enter on the Execution of his Office, he shall take the following Oath or Affirmation: — "I do solemnly swear (or affirm) that I will faithfully execute the Office of President of the United States, and will to the best of my Ability, preserve, protect and defend the Constitution of the United States."

Section 2.

The President shall be Commander in Chief of the Army and Navy of the United States, and of the Militia of the several States, when called into the actual Service of the United States; he may require the Opinion, in writing, of the principal Officer in each of the executive Departments, upon any Subject relating to the Duties of their respective Offices, and he shall have Power to grant Reprieves and Pardons for Offences against the United States, except in Cases of Impeachment.

Section 1. (cont.)

The President must swear this Oath or Affirmation before taking office:

"I do solemnly swear (or affirm) that I will faithfully execute the Office of President of the United States, and will to the best of my Ability, preserve, protect and defend the Constitution of the United States."

Section 2. *Powers of the President.*

The President is the Commander-in-Chief of the Army and the Navy of the United States. He is Commander-in-Chief of those State Militias called into actual service of the United States.

The President may order the heads of each Department to write reports on any subject related to their responsibilities.

The President can reduce Federal criminal sentences and pardon Federal crimes, except in impeachment cases.

Section 2. (cont.)

He shall have Power, by and with the Advice and Consent of the Senate, to make Treaties, provided two thirds of the Senators present concur; and he shall nominate, and by and with the Advice and Consent of the Senate, shall appoint Ambassadors, other public Ministers and Consuls, Judges of the supreme Court, and all other Officers of the United States, whose Appointments are not herein otherwise provided for, and which shall be established by Law: but the Congress may by Law vest the Appointment of such inferior Officers, as they think proper, in the President alone, in the Courts of Law, or in the Heads of Departments.

The President shall have Power to fill up all Vacancies that may happen during the Recess of the Senate, by granting Commissions which shall expire at the End of their next Session.

Section 2. (cont.)

The President can negotiate treaties with foreign coun-tries. He must consult with and get the approval of the Senate by a two-thirds vote.

The President nominates ambassadors and other dip-lomats, Supreme Court Judges, and all other Federal officials created by Law whose appointments are not described in this Constitution elsewhere. He must consult with and get the approval of the Senate to appoint those nominees.

Congress can by Law give the power to appoint lower-level Federal officials, without Senate approval, to either the President, the Courts, or the heads of Depart-ments.

When the Senate is in recess, the President can make appointments to fill vacancies. Those appointments expire at the end of their next Session.

Section 3.

He shall from time to time give to the Congress Information of the State of the Union, and recommend to their Consideration such Measures as he shall judge necessary and expedient; he may, on extraordinary Occasions, convene both Houses, or either of them, and in Case of Disagreement between them, with Respect to the Time of Adjournment, he may adjourn them to such Time as he shall think proper; he shall receive Ambassadors and other public Ministers; he shall take Care that the Laws be faithfully executed, and shall Commission all the Officers of the United States.

Section 4.

The President, Vice President and all civil Officers of the United States, shall be removed from Office on Impeachment for, and Conviction of, Treason, Bribery, or other high Crimes and Misdemeanors.

Section 3. *Responsibilities of the President.*

The President must inform Congress on the State of the Union from time to time.

The President can recommend laws to Congress he believes are necessary or practical.

The President may call one or both Houses of Congress into Session, but only in extraordinary circumstances.

The President may adjourn the Houses of Congress, but only when the two Houses disagree about when to adjourn.

The President can receive ambassadors and other diplomats of foreign countries.

The President must enforce the laws in good faith.

Section 4. *Impeachment and Removal.*

The President, Vice President, and all civil Federal officials can be impeached for Treason, bribery, or other crimes and misbehavior relating to their responsibilities. If convicted, they are removed from office.

Article III.

Article 3.
The Supreme Court.

Section 1.

The judicial Power of the United States shall be vested in one supreme Court, and in such inferior Courts as the Congress may from time to time ordain and establish. The Judges, both of the supreme and inferior Courts, shall hold their Offices during good Behaviour, and shall, at stated Times, receive for their Services a Compensation, which shall not be diminished during their Continuance in Office.

Section 2.

The judicial Power shall extend to all Cases, in Law and Equity, arising under this Constitution, the Laws of the United States, and Treaties made, or which shall be made, under their Authority;

— to all Cases affecting Ambassadors, other public Ministers and Consuls;
— to all Cases of admiralty and maritime Jurisdiction;
— to Controversies to which the United States shall be a Party;

Section 1. *Grant of Power and the Court System.*

The Power to decide cases and interpret the law belongs to the one Supreme Court and to the lower Courts. Congress can establish the lower Courts from time to time.

Judges of both the Supreme Court and the lower Courts are appointed for life terms. They are paid for their services. The amount they are paid cannot be decreased during their term.

Section 2. *Powers of the Courts.*

The Power to decide cases and interpret the law covers only those cases:

- that arise under this Constitution;
- that arise under Federal law;
- that arise under treaties made, or which will be made by, the United States;
- that affect ambassadors or other diplomats of foreign countries;
- that involve the law of the sea;
- that involve the United States as a party;

Section 2. (cont.)

— to Controversies between two or more States;

— between a State and Citizens of another State;

— between Citizens of different States;

— between Citizens of the same State claiming Lands under Grants of different States, and between a State, or the Citizens thereof, and foreign States, Citizens or Subjects.

In all Cases affecting Ambassadors, other public Ministers and Consuls, and those in which a State shall be Party, the supreme Court shall have original Jurisdiction.

In all the other Cases before mentioned, the supreme Court shall have appellate Jurisdiction, both as to Law and Fact, with such Exceptions, and under such Regulations as the Congress shall make.

The Trial of all Crimes, except in Cases of Impeachment, shall be by Jury; and such Trial shall be held in the State where the said Crimes shall have been committed; but when not committed within any State, the Trial shall be at such Place or Places as the Congress may by Law have directed.

Section 2. (cont.)

- between two or more States;

- between a State and citizens of another State;

- between citizens of different States;

- between citizens of the same State claiming different States granted each of them the same land;
- between a State, or Citizens of that State, and foreign countries, citizens, or subjects. Amendment 11, ratified February 7, 1795

For cases involving ambassadors or other diplomats, or for cases where a State is a party, the Supreme Court can hear original trials.

For all other cases listed above, the Supreme Court can hear appeals from trials, on questions of both law and fact. Congress can make exceptions to, and rules for, those appeals.

All criminal trials must be jury trials, except for impeach-ment cases. Trials must be held in the State where the crime was committed. Congress can decide by Law where trials are held for crimes that are not committed in any State.

Section 3.

Treason against the United States shall consist only in levying War against them, or in adhering to their Enemies, giving them Aid and Comfort. No Person shall be convicted of Treason unless on the Testimony of two Witnesses to the same overt Act, or on Confession in open Court.

The Congress shall have Power to declare the Punishment of Treason, but no Attainder of Treason shall work Corruption of Blood, or Forfeiture except during the Life of the Person attainted.

Section 3. *Treason.*

Treason against the United States is defined only as:

* waging war against the United States, or
* supporting the enemies of the United States and giving them aid and comfort.

A person cannot be convicted of Treason unless they commit some overt act. Two witnesses must testify to the same overt act, or that person can confess in open court.

Congress decides the punishment for Treason. The punishment cannot extend to the traitor's family or bar the right to pass an inheritance. The punishment cannot require forfeiting property except during the lifetime of the traitor.

Article IV.

Article 4.
The Relationship of the States.

Section 1.

Full Faith and Credit shall be given in each State to the public Acts, Records, and judicial Proceedings of every other State. And the Congress may by general Laws prescribe the Manner in which such Acts, Records and Proceedings shall be proved, and the Effect thereof.

Section 2.

The Citizens of each State shall be entitled to all Privileges and Immunities of Citizens in the several States.

A Person charged in any State with Treason, Felony, or other Crime, who shall flee from Justice, and be found in another State, shall on Demand of the executive Authority of the State from which he fled, be delivered up, to be removed to the State having Jurisdiction of the Crime.

No Person held to Service or Labour in one State, under the Laws thereof, escaping into another, shall, in Consequence of any Law or Regulation therein, be discharged from such Service or Labour, but shall be delivered up on Claim of the Party to whom such Service or Labour may be due.

Section 1. *Treatment of Other States' Laws.*

Each State must respect and honor each other State's public laws, records, and judicial decisions.

Congress can by general Law decide the effect of those public laws, records, and judicial decisions, and how to prove them in court.

Section 2. *Treatment of Other States' Citizens.*

Citizens of each State are entitled to all the rights and protections of citizenship in other States.

A State must turn over a fugitive from another State on demand of the Governor of that State. This applies to those charged with Treason, a Felony, or another crime in one State who flee to another State.

A slave or indentured servant in one State who escapes to another State cannot be freed under the laws of the second State. If the slave's master files a claim with that State, the State must deliver the slave to the master.
Amendment 13, ratified December 6, 1865

Section 3.

New States may be admitted by the Congress into this Union; but no new State shall be formed or erected within the Jurisdiction of any other State; nor any State be formed by the Junction of two or more States, or Parts of States, without the Consent of the Legislatures of the States concerned as well as of the Congress.

The Congress shall have Power to dispose of and make all needful Rules and Regulations respecting the Territory or other Property belonging to the United States; and nothing in this Constitution shall be so construed as to Prejudice any Claims of the United States, or of any particular State.

Section 4.

The United States shall guarantee to every State in this Union a Republican Form of Government, and shall protect each of them against Invasion; and on Application of the Legislature, or of the Executive (when the Legislature cannot be convened), against domestic Violence.

Section 3. *New States.*

Congress can admit new States into the Union.

Without approval from Congress and the States involved, a new State cannot be formed within any other State, or by joining two States or parts of two States.

Congress can control and make laws regarding the land and other property of the United States.

Nothing in this Constitution affects any current land claims of the United States or any one State.

Section 4. *The Federal Government and the States.*

The United States guarantees to every State a republican form of government.

The United States will protect every State from invasion.

The United States will protect a State against internal violence when called by that State's Legislature. The Governor of that State can call for protection if the State's Legislature cannot.

Article V.

Article 5.
Amending the Constitution.

The Congress, whenever two thirds of both Houses shall deem it necessary, shall propose Amendments to this Constitution, or, on the Application of the Legislatures of two thirds of the several States, shall call a Convention for proposing Amendments, which, in either Case, shall be valid to all Intents and Purposes, as Part of this Constitution, when ratified by the Legislatures of three fourths of the several States, or by Conventions in three fourths thereof, as the one or the other Mode of Ratification may be proposed by the Congress; Provided that no Amendment which may be made prior to the Year One thousand eight hundred and eight shall in any Manner affect the first and fourth Clauses in the Ninth Section of the first Article; and that no State, without its Consent, shall be deprived of its equal Suffrage in the Senate.

Amendments can be proposed either by Congress or by a Convention. Congress can propose an Amendment only with a two-thirds vote of both Houses. Congress must call a Constitutional Convention for proposing Amendments upon a petition from two-thirds of the States.

A proposed Amendment becomes a part of the Constitution, and valid for all intents and purposes, when ratified by three-fourths of the States. A proposed Amendment can be ratified through one of two modes, as decided by Congress:

- approval by the State Legislatures of three-fourths of the States, or

- approval through Conventions held in three-fourths of the States.

No Amendments made before the year 1808 can affect the first and fourth Clauses of Article 1, Section 9. (see pages 30 and 32)

No Amendments can deny a State of its equal vote in the Senate without that State's approval.

Article VI.

Article 6.
Supremacy.

All Debts contracted and Engagements entered into, before the Adoption of this Constitution, shall be as valid against the United States under this Constitution, as under the Confederation. This Constitution, and the Laws of the United States which shall be made in Pursuance thereof; and all Treaties made, or which shall be made, under the Authority of the United States, shall be the supreme Law of the Land; and the Judges in every State shall be bound thereby, any Thing in the Constitution or Laws of any State to the Contrary notwithstanding.

The Senators and Representatives before mentioned, and the Members of the several State Legislatures, and all executive and judicial Officers, both of the United States and of the several States, shall be bound by Oath or Affirmation, to support this Constitution; but no religious Test shall ever be required as a Qualification to any Office or public Trust under the United States.

All debts and agreements of the United States that were valid before this Constitution was adopted remain valid, as they were under the Confederation.

This Constitution is the Supreme Law of the Land, together with all the laws that will be made under it, and all treaties made, or that will be made, by the United States.

State Judges must follow the Constitution, despite anything conflicting in their State's Constitution or laws.

All officials must swear to support this Constitution. This includes: Senators, Representatives, Members of State Legislatures, all Federal and State officials, and all Federal and State judges.

No religious test will ever be required of someone to hold Federal office.

Article VII.

Article 7.
Ratification.

The Ratification of the Conventions of nine States, shall be sufficient for the Establishment of this Constitution between the States so ratifying the Same.

Each State will hold a Convention to vote on ratifying this Constitution. If at least nine states ratify, the Constitution is adopted. The Constitution applies only between those States that ratify it.

Amendments

Bill of Rights.

Bill of Rights.

Amendment I.

Congress shall make no law respecting an establishment of religion, or prohibiting the free exercise thereof; or abridging the freedom of speech, or of the press; or the right of the people peaceably to assemble, and to petition the Government for a redress of grievances.

Amendment II.

A well regulated Militia, being necessary to the security of a free State, the right of the people to keep and bear Arms, shall not be infringed.

Amendment III.

No Soldier shall, in time of peace be quartered in any house, without the consent of the Owner, nor in time of war, but in a manner to be prescribed by law.

Amendment 1. *Right to Free Expression.*
Ratified December 15, 1791

Congress will not make any law:

- establishing a national religion.
- banning the free exercise of religion.
- limiting the freedom of speech.
- limiting the freedom of the press.
- limiting the right of the people to peacefully assemble.
- limiting the right to petition the government.

Amendment 2. *Right to Bear Arms.*
Ratified December 15, 1791

A well regulated Militia, being necessary to the security of a free State, the right of the people to keep and bear Arms shall not be infringed.

Amendment 3. *Private Stationing of Soldiers.*
Ratified December 15, 1791

During peacetime, soldiers cannot be stationed in any house without the owner's approval. During wartime, they can be, but only by Law.

Amendment IV.

The right of the people to be secure in their persons, houses, papers, and effects, against unreasonable searches and seizures, shall not be violated, and no Warrants shall issue, but upon probable cause, supported by Oath or affirmation, and particularly describing the place to be searched, and the persons or things to be seized.

Amendment V.

No person shall be held to answer for a capital, or otherwise infamous crime, unless on a presentment or indictment of a Grand Jury, except in cases arising in the land or naval forces, or in the Militia, when in actual service in time of War or public danger; nor shall any person be subject for the same offence to be twice put in jeopardy of life or limb; nor shall be compelled in any criminal case to be a witness against himself, nor be deprived of life, liberty, or property, without due process of law; nor shall private property be taken for public use, without just compensation.

Amendment 4. *Security from Government.*
Ratified December 15, 1791

The right of the people to be free from unreasonable searches and seizures of their bodies and property will not be violated.

Warrants can only be issued if:

- based on probable cause,
- supported by sworn testimony, and
- specifically describing the place to be searched, and the persons or things to be seized.

Amendment 5. *Right to Fair Procedures.*
Ratified December 15, 1791

No one will be:

- charged with or held for a crime punishable by death or imprisonment unless first indicted by a Grand Jury, except in military cases during wartime or public danger.
- tried twice for the same crime.
- forced to incriminate themselves.
- denied their life, liberty, or property without fair procedures.

Private property can only be taken for public use with fair payment.

Amendment VI.

In all criminal prosecutions, the accused shall enjoy the right to a speedy and public trial, by an impartial jury of the State and district wherein the crime shall have been committed, which district shall have been previously ascertained by law, and to be informed of the nature and cause of the accusation; to be confronted with the witnesses against him; to have compulsory process for obtaining witnesses in his favor, and to have the Assistance of Counsel for his defence.

Amendment VII.

In Suits at common law, where the value in controversy shall exceed twenty dollars, the right of trial by jury shall be preserved, and no fact tried by a jury, shall be otherwise re-examined in any Court of the United States, than according to the rules of the common law.

Amendment 6. *Right to Fair Criminal Trial.*
Ratified December 15, 1791

People accused of crimes have the right:

- to a speedy and public jury trial.
- to an impartial jury from the State and district where the crime happened, with the district determined by Law.
- to be informed of the nature and cause of the charges against them.
- to face and question the witnesses against them.
- to call favorable witnesses to testify.
- to a lawyer to help in their defense.

Amendment 7. *Right to Jury Trial.*
Ratified December 15, 1791

In civil cases:

- the right to a jury trial is protected in cases over more than twenty dollars.
- Federal Courts can re-examine a jury's decision on questions of fact only under common law rules.

Amendment VIII.

Excessive bail shall not be required, nor excessive fines imposed, nor cruel and unusual punishments inflicted.

Amendment IX.

The enumeration in the Constitution, of certain rights, shall not be construed to deny or disparage others retained by the people.

Amendment X.

The powers not delegated to the United States by the Constitution, nor prohibited by it to the States, are reserved to the States respectively, or to the people.

Amendment 8. *Right to Fair Punishment.*
Ratified December 15, 1791

Excessive bail will not be required. Excessive fines will not be imposed. Cruel and unusual punishment will not be inflicted.

Amendment 9. *Rights Not Listed.*
Ratified December 15, 1791

The listing of rights in this Constitution does not deny or limit other rights held by the people.

Amendment 10. *Powers Not Listed.*
Ratified December 15, 1791

If a power is not given to the United States or denied to the States by this Constitution, then it is reserved to the States or to the people.

Civil War Amendments.

Civil War Amendments.

Amendment XIII.

Section 1.

Neither slavery nor involuntary servitude, except as a punishment for crime whereof the party shall have been duly convicted, shall exist within the United States, or any place subject to their jurisdiction.

Section 2.

Congress shall have power to enforce this article by appropriate legislation.

Amendment 13. *Slavery.*
Ratified December 6, 1865

Section 1.

Slavery and involuntary servitude are banned, except as punishment following conviction for a crime. This applies within the United States and any place subject to its jurisdiction.

Section 2.

Congress can make laws to enforce this Amendment.

Amendment XIV.

Section 1.

All persons born or naturalized in the United States, and subject to the jurisdiction thereof, are citizens of the United States and of the State wherein they reside. No State shall make or enforce any law which shall abridge the privileges or immunities of citizens of the United States; nor shall any State deprive any person of life, liberty, or property, without due process of law; nor deny to any person within its jurisdiction the equal protection of the laws.

Amendment 14. *Citizenship.*

Ratified July 9, 1868

Section 1.

All people subject to the jurisdiction of the United States and who were born in, or became citizens by Law in, the United States are citizens of the United States and of the State where they live.

States cannot make or enforce any law which denies or limits the rights and protections of United States citizens.

States cannot deny any person of life, liberty, or property without fair procedures.

States cannot deny the equal protection of the laws to anyone subject to their jurisdiction.

Amendment XIV. (cont.)

Section 2.

Representatives shall be apportioned among the several States according to their respective numbers, counting the whole number of persons in each State, excluding Indians not taxed. But when the right to vote at any election for the choice of electors for President and Vice President of the United States, Representatives in Congress, the Executive and Judicial officers of a State, or the members of the Legislature thereof, is denied to any of the male inhabitants of such State, being twenty-one years of age, and citizens of the United States, or in any way abridged, except for participation in rebellion, or other crime, the basis of representation therein shall be reduced in the proportion which the number of such male citizens shall bear to the whole number of male citizens twenty-one years of age in such State.

Amendment 14. (cont.)

Section 2.

Each State gets Representatives based on its population. A State's population is calculated by counting each person in the State, excluding non-citizen Indians under tribal rule.

If a State denies or limits the right to vote of any men aged twenty-one or older in that State in Elections (except where it is limited because of rebellion or other crime), the number of Representatives that State gets will be lowered based on the ratio of such men in the State to the whole number of men aged twenty-one or older in the State. This applies to Elections for Electors for President and Vice President, Representatives in Congress, State officers and Judges, and members of the State Legislature.

Amendment XIV. (cont.)

Section 3.

No person shall be a Senator or Representative in Congress, or elector of President and Vice President, or hold any office, civil or military, under the United States, or under any State, who, having previously taken an oath, as a member of Congress, or as an officer of the United States, or as a member of any State legislature, or as an executive or judicial officer of any State, to support the Constitution of the United States, shall have engaged in insurrection or rebellion against the same, or given aid or comfort to the enemies thereof. But Congress may by a vote of two-thirds of each House, remove such disability.

Amendment 14. (cont.)

Section 3.

Any person who rebelled against the Constitution after swearing, as a Federal or State official, to support it, cannot be:

- a Senator or Representative,
- an Elector for President or Vice President, or
- a civil or military Federal or State official.

This also applies to those who, after swearing to support the Constitution, gave aid or comfort to the enemies of the United States.

Congress can remove the above restriction from a person with a two-thirds vote of each House.

Amendment XIV. (cont.)

Section 4.

The validity of the public debt of the United States, authorized by law, including debts incurred for payment of pensions and bounties for services in suppressing insurrection or rebellion, shall not be questioned. But neither the United States nor any State shall assume or pay any debt or obligation incurred in aid of insurrection or rebellion against the United States, or any claim for the loss or emancipation of any slave; but all such debts, obligations and claims shall be held illegal and void.

Section 5.

The Congress shall have power to enforce, by appropriate legislation, the provisions of this article.

Amendment 14. (cont.)

Section 4.

The public debt of the United States that was authorized by Law remains valid. This includes debts taken on to pay pensions and bounties for services in suppressing rebellion.

Neither the United States nor any State will pay any debt taken on in support of rebellion against the United States, or any claim for reimbursement for the loss or freedom of any slave. All those debts and claims are illegal and invalid.

Section 5.

Congress can make laws to enforce this Amendment.

Amendment XV.

Section 1.

The right of citizens of the United States to vote shall not be denied or abridged by the United States or by any State on account of race, color, or previous condition of servitude.

Section 2.

The Congress shall have power to enforce this article by appropriate legislation.

Amendment 15. *Voting Rights: Race and Color.*
Ratified February 3, 1870

Section 1.

Neither the United States nor any State can deny or limit the right to vote because of a citizen's race, color, or previous status as slave or servant.

Section 2.

Congress can make laws to enforce this Amendment.

Election Amendments.

Election Amendments.

Amendment XII.

The Electors shall meet in their respective states, and vote by ballot for President and Vice-President, one of whom, at least, shall not be an inhabitant of the same state with themselves; they shall name in their ballots the person voted for as President, and in distinct ballots the person voted for as Vice-President, and they shall make distinct lists of all persons voted for as President, and of all persons voted for as Vice-President, and of the number of votes for each, which lists they shall sign and certify, and transmit sealed to the seat of the government of the United States, directed to the President of the Senate;

— The President of the Senate shall, in the presence of the Senate and House of Representatives, open all the certificates and the votes shall then be counted;

Amendment 12. *Electoral College Update.*

Ratified June 15, 1804

The Electors meet in their States and each Elector votes for President and for Vice President, at least one of whom must live in a different State than that Elector. Each Elector casts a vote for President and a vote for Vice President. The Electors of each State then make two lists, one for President and one for Vice President, of all the persons voted for and the number of votes for each. The Electors then sign each list and send them to the President of the Senate at the capital of the United States.

The President of the Senate will open all the lists and count the votes. This will be done in front of the Senate and the House of Representatives.

Amendment XII. (cont.)

— The person having the greatest number of votes for President, shall be the President, if such number be a majority of the whole number of Electors appointed; and if no person have such majority, then from the persons having the highest numbers not exceeding three on the list of those voted for as President, the House of Representatives shall choose immediately, by ballot, the President. But in choosing the President, the votes shall be taken by states, the representation from each state having one vote; a quorum for this purpose shall consist of a member or members from two-thirds of the states, and a majority of all the states shall be necessary to a choice. And if the House of Representatives shall not choose a President whenever the right of choice shall devolve upon them, before the fourth day of March next following, then the Vice-President shall act as President, as in the case of the death or other constitutional disability of the President.

— The person having the greatest number of votes as Vice-President, shall be the Vice-President, if such number be a majority of the whole number of Electors appointed, and if no person have a majority, then from the two highest numbers on the list, the Senate shall choose the Vice-President; a quorum for the purpose shall consist of two-thirds of the whole number of Senators, and a majority of the whole number shall be necessary to a choice. But no person constitutionally ineligible to the office of President shall be eligible to that of Vice-President of the United States

Amendment 12. (cont.)

The person who gets votes for President from a majority of the Electors, and gets more votes than anyone else, becomes President. If no one gets votes from a majority of the Electors, then the House of Representatives selects the President from among the three people who got the most votes.

Where the House of Representatives selects the President, it must do so by majority vote. The vote is held by State, and the Representatives of a State together have one vote. Representatives from at least two-thirds of the States must be present for the vote. The person who gets votes from a majority of the States becomes the President. If the House of Representatives cannot select a President by the next March 4th, then the Vice President becomes Acting President, as when the President dies or cannot carry out the responsibilities of President.

The person who gets votes for Vice President from a majority of the Electors, and gets more votes than anyone else, becomes Vice President. If no one gets votes from a majority of the Electors, then the Senate selects the Vice President from among the two people who got the most votes. The person who gets votes from a majority of Senators becomes Vice President. At least two-thirds of the Senators must be present for the vote. No one can become Vice President who is unable to become President under the Constitution.

Amendment XVII.

The Senate of the United States shall be composed of two Senators from each State, elected by the people thereof, for six years; and each Senator shall have one vote. The electors in each State shall have the qualifications requisite for electors of the most numerous branch of the State legislatures.

When vacancies happen in the representation of any State in the Senate, the executive authority of such State shall issue writs of election to fill such vacancies: Provided, That the legislature of any State may empower the executive thereof to make temporary appointments until the people fill the vacancies by election as the legislature may direct.

This amendment shall not be so construed as to affect the election or term of any Senator chosen before it becomes valid as part of the Constitution.

Amendment 17. *Direct Election of Senators.*
Ratified April 8, 1913

The Senate is made up of Senators elected for six-year terms by the people of their State. Each State gets two Senators. Each Senator has one vote. Those people who meet the requirements to vote for the largest branch of their State Legislature are qualified to vote for their Senators.

The Governor of a State will order an Election whenever that State has a vacancy in the Senate. State Legislatures can allow the Governor of that State to temporarily appoint a Senator until the people fill the seat in an Election.

This Amendment will not affect the election or term of any Senator elected before it goes into effect as part of the Constitution.

Amendment XX.

Section 1.

The terms of the President and Vice President shall end at noon on the 20th day of January, and the terms of Senators and Representatives at noon on the 3d day of January, of the years in which such terms would have ended if this article had not been ratified; and the terms of their successors shall then begin.

Section 2.

The Congress shall assemble at least once in every year, and such meeting shall begin at noon on the 3d day of January, unless they shall by law appoint a different day.

Amendment 20. *Elected Terms.*

Ratified January 23, 1933

Section 1.

The President and Vice President end their terms at noon on January 20th in the last year of their terms. The Senators and Representatives end their terms at noon on January 3rd in the last year of their terms. The last year of those terms is unchanged by this Amendment and remains as it was before this Amendment was ratified. After those terms end, their successors begin their terms.

Section 2.

Congress must meet at least once a year. That meeting must begin at noon on January 3rd. Congress can choose a different day by Law.

Amendment XX. (cont.)

Section 3.

If, at the time fixed for the beginning of the term of the President, the President elect shall have died, the Vice President elect shall become President. If a President shall not have been chosen before the time fixed for the beginning of his term, or if the President elect shall have failed to qualify, then the Vice President elect shall act as President until a President shall have qualified; and the Congress may by law provide for the case wherein neither a President elect nor a Vice President elect shall have qualified, declaring who shall then act as President, or the manner in which one who is to act shall be selected, and such person shall act accordingly until a President or Vice President shall have qualified.

Section 4.

The Congress may by law provide for the case of the death of any of the persons from whom the House of Representatives may choose a President whenever the right of choice shall have devolved upon them, and for the case of the death of any of the persons from whom the Senate may choose a Vice President whenever the right of choice shall have devolved upon them.

Amendment 20. (cont.)

Section 3.

If the President-Elect dies before his term begins, the Vice President-Elect will become President instead.

If a President has not been selected before the beginning of the next term, or the President-Elect does not qualify for President under the Constitution, then the Vice President-Elect will become Acting President until a qualified President is selected.

Congress can decide by Law what happens when both the President-Elect and Vice President-Elect do not qualify for President under the Constitution. This includes deciding who becomes Acting President and how the Acting President is chosen. That Acting President carries out the responsibilities of President until a qualified President or Vice President is chosen.

Section 4.

Congress can decide by Law what happens if, when the House of Representatives must select the President, one of the people for whom they can vote dies.

Congress can decide by Law what happens if, when the Senate must select the Vice President, one of the people for whom they can vote dies.

Amendment XX. (cont.)

Section 5.

Sections 1 and 2 shall take effect on the 15th day of October following the ratification of this article.

Section 6.

This article shall be inoperative unless it shall have been ratified as an amendment to the Constitution by the legislatures of three-fourths of the several States within seven years from the date of its submission.

Amendment 20. (cont.)

Section 5.

Sections 1 and 2 of this Amendment go into effect on October 15th after this Amendment is ratified.

Section 6.

This Amendment goes into effect only if it is ratified within seven years from when it is first submitted to the States by Congress. It must be ratified by three-fourths of the State Legislatures.

Amendment XXII.

Section 1.

No person shall be elected to the office of the President more than twice, and no person who has held the office of President, or acted as President, for more than two years of a term to which some other person was elected President shall be elected to the office of the President more than once. But this Article shall not apply to any person holding the office of President when this Article was proposed by the Congress, and shall not prevent any person who may be holding the office of President, or acting as President, during the term within which this Article becomes operative from holding the office of President or acting as President during the remainder of such term.

Section 2.

This article shall be inoperative unless it shall have been ratified as an amendment to the Constitution by the legislatures of three-fourths of the several States within seven years from the date of its submission to the States by the Congress.

Amendment 22. *Term Limits of Presidents.*
Ratified February 27, 1951

Section 1.

A person cannot be elected President more than twice.

A person cannot be elected President more than once if they were President or Acting President during the term of someone else elected President. This only applies if that Person was President or Acting President for at least two years during that term.

This Amendment does not apply to whoever is the President when Congress proposed this Amendment. This Amendment will not prevent any President or Acting President during the current term from completing their term.

Section 2.

This Amendment goes into effect only if it is ratified within seven years from when it is first submitted to the States by Congress. It must be ratified by three-fourths of the State Legislatures.

Amendment XXV.

Section 1.

In case of the removal of the President from office or of his death or resignation, the Vice President shall become President.

Section 2.

Whenever there is a vacancy in the office of the Vice President, the President shall nominate a Vice President who shall take office upon confirmation by a majority vote of both Houses of Congress.

Section 3.

Whenever the President transmits to the President pro tempore of the Senate and the Speaker of the House of Representatives his written declaration that he is unable to discharge the powers and duties of his office, and until he transmits to them a written declaration to the contrary, such powers and duties shall be discharged by the Vice President as Acting President

Amendment 25. *Succession of Presidents.*
Ratified February 10, 1967

Section 1.

If the President is removed from office, dies, or resigns, the Vice President becomes President.

Section 2.

Whenever there is no Vice President, the President nominates a Vice President. The nominee takes office only if approved by a majority vote of both Houses of Congress.

Section 3.

The President can send written notice to the President pro tempore of the Senate and the Speaker of the House that he is unable to carry out the responsibilities of President. If he does, the Vice President becomes Acting President until the President sends them written notice that he is now able to carry out the responsibilities of President.

Amendment XXV. (cont.)

Section 4.

Whenever the Vice President and a majority of either the principal officers of the executive departments or of such other body as Congress may by law provide, transmit to the President pro tempore of the Senate and the Speaker of the House of Representatives their written declaration that the President is unable to discharge the powers and duties of his office, the Vice President shall immediately assume the powers and duties of the office as Acting President.

Amendment 25. (cont.)

Section 4.

The Vice President can send written notice to the President pro tempore of the Senate and the Speaker of the House that the President is unable to carry out his responsibilities as President. A majority of the heads of the Departments, or some other similar group Congress decides by Law, must join the statement. Once the statement is sent, the Vice President becomes Acting President.

Amendment XXV. (cont.)

Section 4. (cont.)

Thereafter, when the President transmits to the President pro tempore of the Senate and the Speaker of the House of Representatives his written declaration that no inability exists, he shall resume the powers and duties of his office unless the Vice President and a majority of either the principal officers of the executive department or of such other body as Congress may by law provide, transmit within four days to the President pro tempore of the Senate and the Speaker of the House of Representatives their written declaration that the President is unable to discharge the powers and duties of his office. Thereupon Congress shall decide the issue, assembling within forty-eight hours for that purpose if not in session. If the Congress, within twenty-one days after receipt of the latter written declaration, or, if Congress is not in session, within twenty-one days after Congress is required to assemble, determines by two-thirds vote of both Houses that the President is unable to discharge the powers and duties of his office, the Vice President shall continue to discharge the same as Acting President; otherwise, the President shall resume the powers and duties of his office.

Amendment 25. (cont.)

Section 4. (cont.)

Afterwards, if the President sends written notice to the President pro tempore of the Senate and the Speaker of the House that he is not unable to carry out his responsibilities as President, then he resumes his responsibilities as President.

Within four days after the President sends his written notice, the Vice President can send written notice to the President pro tempore and the Speaker of the House that the President is still unable to carry out his responsibilities as President. A majority of the heads of the Departments, or some other similar group Congress decides by Law, must join the statement. If Congress is not in Session, they must call a Session within forty-eight hours. Congress has twenty-one days after receiving this notice, or after coming into Session if they were not already in Session, to decide.

If Congress decides by a two-thirds vote that the President is unable to carry out his responsibilities as President, then the Vice President remains Acting President. Otherwise, the President resumes his responsibilities as President.

Voting Rights.

Voting Rights.

Amendment XIX.

The right of citizens of the United States to vote shall not be denied or abridged by the United States or by any State on account of sex.

Congress shall have power to enforce this article by appropriate legislation.

Amendment 19. *Voting Rights: Sex.*
Ratified August 18, 1920

Neither the United States nor any State can deny or limit the right to vote because of a citizen's sex.

Congress can make laws to enforce this Amendment.

Amendment XXIII.

Section 1.

The District constituting the seat of Government of the United States shall appoint in such manner as the Congress may direct:

A number of electors of President and Vice President equal to the whole number of Senators and Representatives in Congress to which the District would be entitled if it were a State, but in no event more than the least populous State; they shall be in addition to those appointed by the States, but they shall be considered, for the purposes of the election of President and Vice President, to be electors appointed by a State; and they shall meet in the District and perform such duties as provided by the twelfth article of amendment.

Section 2.

The Congress shall have power to enforce this article by appropriate legislation.

Amendment 23. *The Capitol District.*

Ratified March 29, 1961

Section 1.

The District that is the capitol of the United States appoints a number of Electors for President and Vice President. Congress can decide how the District appoints its Electors. The District gets Electors equal to the number of Senators added to the number of Representatives that the District would have if it were a State. The District cannot have more Electors than the State with the lowest population. The Electors from the District are considered Electors appointed by a State when voting for President and Vice President. The Electors from the District meet in the District and perform the duties required of Electors by the Twelfth Amendment.

Section 2.

Congress can make laws to enforce this Amendment.

Amendment XXIV.

Section 1.

The right of citizens of the United States to vote in any primary or other election for President or Vice President, for electors for President or Vice President, or for Senator or Representative in Congress, shall not be denied or abridged by the United States or any State by reason of failure to pay any poll tax or other tax.

Section 2.

The Congress shall have power to enforce this article by appropriate legislation.

Amendment XXVI.

Section 1.

The right of citizens of the United States, who are eighteen years of age or older, to vote shall not be denied or abridged by the United States or by any State on account of age.

Section 2.

The Congress shall have power to enforce this article by appropriate legislation.

132

Amendment 24. *Voting Rights: Poll Taxes.*
Ratified January 23, 1964

Section 1.

Neither the United States nor any State can deny or limit the right to vote because of a citizen's failure to pay taxes. This applies to all Elections for President, Vice President, Senators or Representatives, including primaries.

Section 2.

Congress can make laws to enforce this Amendment.

Amendment 26. *Voting Rights: Age.*
Ratified July 1, 1971

Section 1.

Neither the United States nor any State can deny or limit the right to vote because of a citizen's age. This applies only to citizens aged eighteen or older.

Section 2.

Congress can make laws to enforce this Amendment

Alcohol, Taxes, and Other.

Alcohol, Taxes, and Other.

Amendment XI.

The Judicial power of the United States shall not be construed to extend to any suit in law or equity, commenced or prosecuted against one of the United States by Citizens of another State, or by Citizens or Subjects of any Foreign State.

Amendment XVI.

The Congress shall have power to lay and collect taxes on incomes, from whatever source derived, without apportionment among the several States, and without regard to any census or enumeration.

Amendment 11. *State Immunity.*
Ratified February 7, 1795

Federal Courts cannot hear cases:

* against one of the States by citizens of another State.
* against one of the States by citizens or subjects of a foreign country.

Amendment 16. *Incomes Taxes.*
Rati ied February 3, 1913

Congress can impose and collect income tax covering any income source. Congress does not need to tax in proportion to a State's population or consider the Census or any population calculation when imposing or collecting an income tax.

Amendment XVIII.

Section 1.

After one year from the ratification of this article the manufacture, sale, or transportation of intoxicating liquors within, the importation thereof into, or the exportation thereof from the United States and all territory subject to the jurisdiction thereof for beverage purposes is hereby prohibited.

Section 2.

The Congress and the several States shall have concurrent power to enforce this article by appropriate legislation.

Section 3.

This article shall be inoperative unless it shall have been ratified as an amendment to the Constitution by the legislatures of the several States, as provided in the Constitution, within seven years from the date of the submission hereof to the States by the Congress.

Amendment 18. *Prohibition of Alcohol.*
Ratified January 16, 1919

Section 1.

One year after this Amendment is ratified, it is illegal to make, sell, transport, or import alcoholic drinks. This applies within the United States and any territory subject to its jurisdiction.

Section 2.

Congress and each State can make laws to enforce this Amendment.

Section 3.

This Amendment goes into effect only if it is ratified within seven years from when it is first submitted to the States by Congress. It must be ratified by the State Legislatures as described in the Constitution. Amendment 21, ratified December 5, 1933

Amendment XXI.

Section 1.

The eighteenth article of amendment to the Constitution of the United States is hereby repealed.

Section 2.

The transportation or importation into any State, Territory, or possession of the United States for delivery or use therein of intoxicating liquors, in violation of the laws thereof, is hereby prohibited.

Section 3.

This article shall be inoperative unless it shall have been ratified as an amendment to the Constitution by conventions in the several States, as provided in the Constitution, within seven years from the date of the submission hereof to the States by the Congress.

Amendment XXVII.

No law, varying the compensation for the services of the Senators and Representatives, shall take effect, until an election of Representatives shall have intervened.

Amendment 21. *Repeal of the 18th Amendment.*
Ratified December 5, 1933

Section 1.

The Eighteenth Amendment is repealed.

Section 2.

States, territories, and other possessions of the United States can by Law make illegal the transport or import of alcoholic drinks.

Section 3.

This Amendment goes into effect only if it is ratified within seven years from when it is first submitted to the States by Congress. It must be ratified by Conventions in the States as described in the Constitution.

Amendment 27. *Pay of Congressmen.*
Ratified May 5, 1992

No law can go into effect that changes the pay of Senators and Representatives until after the next election of Representatives.

"While a constitution may set forth rights and liberties, only the citizens can maintain and guarantee those freedoms. Active and informed citizenship is not just a right; it is a duty."

-Ronald Reagan

About the Author

James Madison Jr. is credited as the "Father of the Constitution." After drafting the document, he wrote a series of papers arguing for its adoption under the penname "Publius," together with Alexander Hamilton and John Jay. He was a proud Virginian, and he was elected the 4th President of the United States in 1809. He died in 1836.

About the Editor

M.J. Wawz is an attorney, strategist, and investor. He writes about life and the law under this pseudonym. He is from Chicago, and now lives elsewhere.

www.ingramcontent.com/pod-product-compliance
Lightning Source LLC
Chambersburg PA
CBHW072048280526
45788CB00006B/2230